NEIL YOUNG
COMPLETE MUSIC
VOLUME III
[1974-1979]

DISCOGRAPHY

On The Beach — 7/74
Reprise-K54014
Tonight's The Night — 5/75
(with Crazy Horse)
Reprise-K54040
Zuma — 11/75
(with Crazy Horse)
Reprise-K54057
Long May You Run — 9/76
Reprise-K54081
Reissued Reprise-MS2253
American Stars 'N' Bars — 6/77
Reprise-K54088
Decade — 12/77
Reprise-K64037
Comes A Time — 7/78
Reprise-K54090
Rust Never Sleeps — 10/79
(with Crazy Horse)
Reprise-K54105

Photography:
Joel Bernstein: Pages 4, 43, 106, 148, 163, 164, 165, 186, 201.
Henry Diltz: Cover, pages 80, 81, 122.
Art Direction: Neil Young
Design & Coordination: Tommy Steele

CONTENTS

ON THE BEACH

On the way to San Luis Obispo
for a benefit playing with the Eagles,
1974.

ABOUT TO RAIN

Words and Music by
NEIL YOUNG

See the sky a-bout ___ to rain, bro-ken clouds and rain; ___ lo-co-mo-tive, pull ___ the train,

Some are bound for hap - pi - ness, some are bound to glo-

ry; some are bound to live___ with less,

'who can tell your sto - ry? See the sky a - bout___

_ to rain,___ bro-ken clouds and rain;__ lo-co-mo-tive, pull__

ON THE BEACH

Words and Music by
NEIL YOUNG

REVOLUTION BLUES

Words and Music by
NEIL YOUNG

and in this land of con-di-tions, I'm
is full of fa-mous stars,

not a-bove_ sus-pi-cion; I won't at-
but I hate_ them worse than lep-ers and

To Coda

tack you, but I won't_ back you._
I'll kill them in_ their cars._

Well, it's so good to be_ here_ a-sleep on your lawn._

Re-mem-ber your guard dog?_ Well, I'm a-fraid that he's gone._ It was

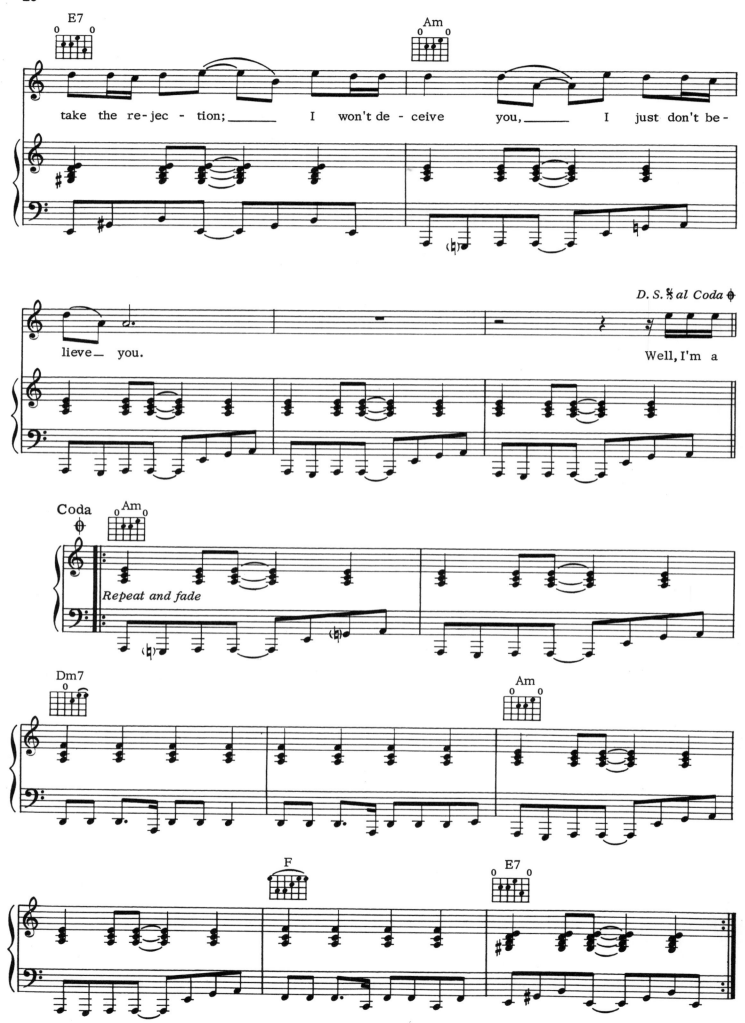

WALK ON

Words and Music by
NEIL YOUNG

hear some people been talkin' me down,
I re-mem-ber the good old days,

bring up my name, pass it 'round.
stayed up all night get-tin' crazed.

MOTION PICTURES

Words and Music by
NEIL YOUNG

FOR THE TURNSTILES

Words and Music by
NEIL YOUNG

VAMPIRE BLUES

Words and Music by
NEIL YOUNG

AMBULANCE BLUES

Words and Music by
NEIL YOUNG

* Guitarists: Tune all strings down one whole step.

TONIGHT'S THE NIGHT

Backstage at
the Roxy, 1973.

TONIGHT'S THE NIGHT

Words and Music by
NEIL YOUNG

SPEAKIN' OUT

Words and Music by
NEIL YOUNG

WORLD ON A STRING

Words and Music by
NEIL YOUNG

You know I lose, you know I win;
an - swer is not un - known,

you know I call for the shape I'm in.
I'm search-in', search - in', and how I've grown.

BORROWED TUNE

Words and Music by
NEIL YOUNG

COME ON BABY LET'S GO DOWNTOWN

Words and Music by
DANNY WHITTEN and NEIL YOUNG

Moderate Rock beat

Come on, ba - by, let's go down - town,_ let's go, let's go, let's go down - town._

Come on, ba - by, let me

MELLOW MY MIND

Words and Music by
NEIL YOUNG

ROLL ANOTHER NUMBER

Words and Music by
NEIL YOUNG

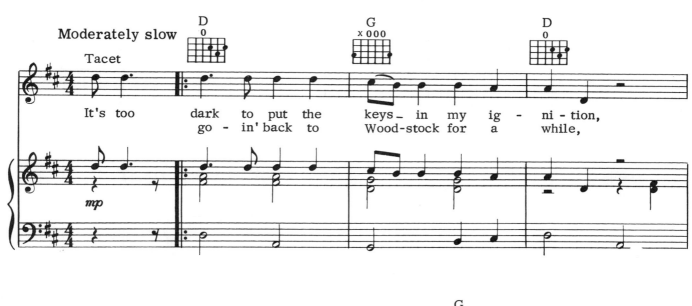

It's too dark to put the keys — in my ig - ni - tion,
go - in' back to Wood-stock for a while,

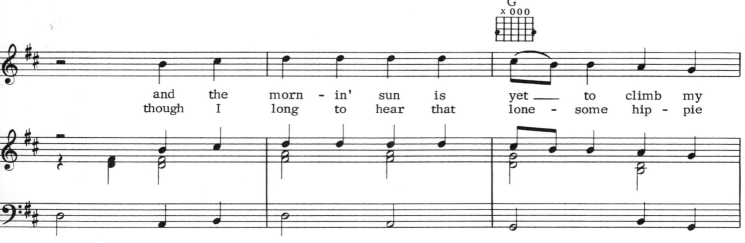

and the morn - in' sun is yet — to climb my
though I long to hear is that lone - some hip - pie

hood or - na - ment.
smile.
But be - fore too long I
I'm a mil - lion miles a -

67

ALBUQUERQUE

Words and Music by
NEIL YOUNG

Well, they say that San-ta Fe is less than nine-ty miles a-way, and I got time to roll a num-ber and rent a car. Oh,— Al - bu-

NEW MAMA

Words and Music by
NEIL YOUNG

Moderately slow, in 2

New ma - ma's got a son in her eye;

LOOKOUT JOE

Words and Music by
NEIL YOUNG

Moderate Gospel beat

TIRED EYES

Words and Music by
NEIL YOUNG

ZUMA

On Zuma Beach
with Crazy Horse, 1975.

DON'T CRY NO TEARS

Words and Music by
NEIL YOUNG

PARDON MY HEART

Words and Music by
NEIL YOUNG

DANGER BIRD

Words and Music by
NEIL YOUNG

Slowly, in 2

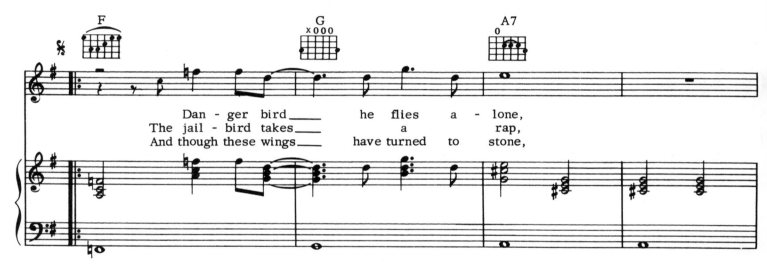

Dan - ger bird____ he flies a - lone,
The jail - bird takes____ a rap,
And though these wings____ have turned to stone,

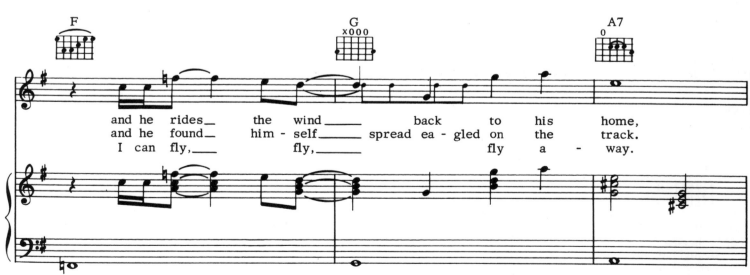

and he rides____ the wind____ back to his home,
and he found____ him - self____ spread ea - gled on the track.
I can fly,____ fly,____ fly a - way.

There you are and here I am.
when I left you far be - hind.

Fly, fly, fly.

Repeat and fade

Repeat and fade

LOOKIN' FOR A LOVE

Words and Music by
NEIL YOUNG

BARSTOOL BLUES

Words and Music by
NEIL YOUNG

STUPID GIRL

Words and Music by
NEIL YOUNG

You're such a stu-pid girl. _____ I saw you in Mer -

You're such a stu-pid girl; _

you're such a stu-pid girl. _____

DRIVE BACK

Words and Music by
NEIL YOUNG

CORTEZ THE KILLER

Words and Music by
NEIL YOUNG

He came

danc - ing a-cross the wa - ter with his gal - le - ons___ and guns,___
sub - jects gath - ered 'round__ him, like the leaves a - round__ the tree,___

THROUGH MY SAILS

Words and Music by
NEIL YOUNG

LONG MAY YOU RUN

Watching Beach Boys perform,
CSNY Tour 1974,
Mile High Stadium, Denver.

LONG MAY YOU RUN

Words and Music by
NEIL YOUNG

With your chrome heart shin - in' in the sun,

long may you run. ___

1.

Well, it was

2.

3.

LET IT SHINE

Words and Music by
NEIL YOUNG

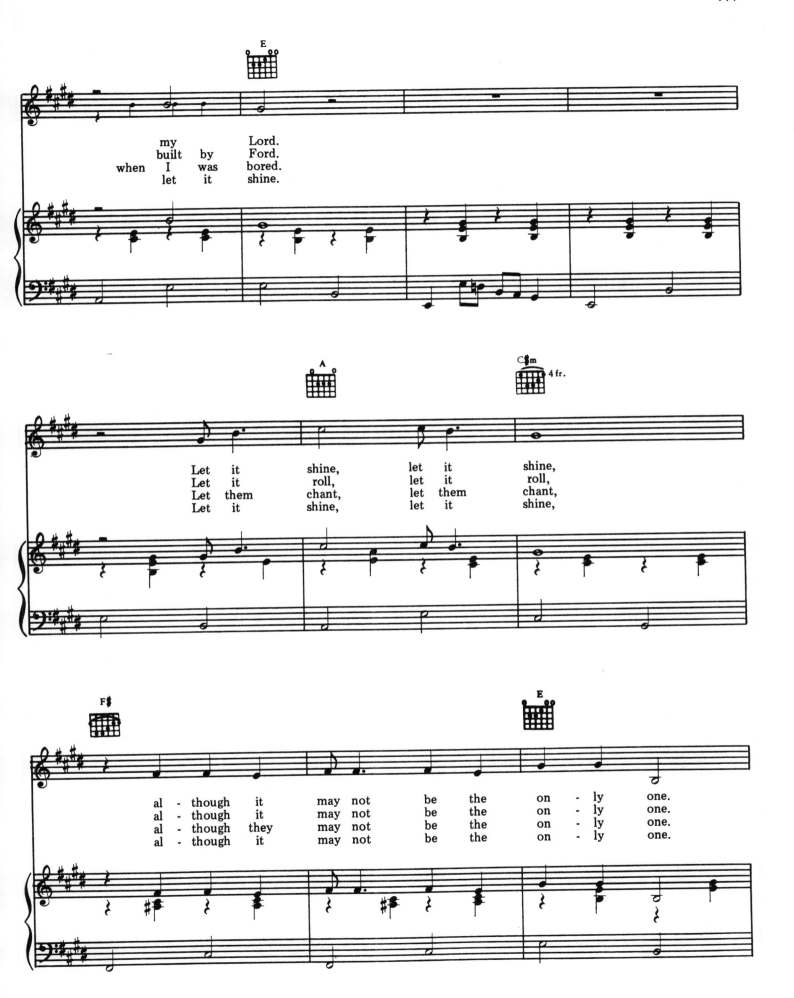

MIDNIGHT ON THE BAY

Words and Music by
NEIL YOUNG

Moderately slow, in 2

It's mid-night on the bay_____ and lights are
What's this I see?_____ There's some-one
mid-night on the bay,_____ lights are

shin - in'_____ and the sail - boats sway;_____
com - in',_____ walk - in' right up to me._____
shin - in'_____ on the sail - boats that sway_____

OCEAN GIRL

Words and Music by
NEIL YOUNG

FONTAINEBLEAU

Words and Music by
NEIL YOUNG

Moderately, with a beat

Who put the palm o-ver my blonde? Who put all the tar on the

morn-ing sand?__ Who took ev-'ry-thing from where__ it once was and

put it where it last was seen?__ Fon-taine-bleau,__ they paint-ed it green,__ Fon-taine-bleau__

__ for the well-to-do__ at the Fon-taine-bleau.__

**AMERICAN STARS
'N' BARS**
Forum, Los Angeles, 1976.

LIKE A HURRICANE

Words and Music by
NEIL YOUNG

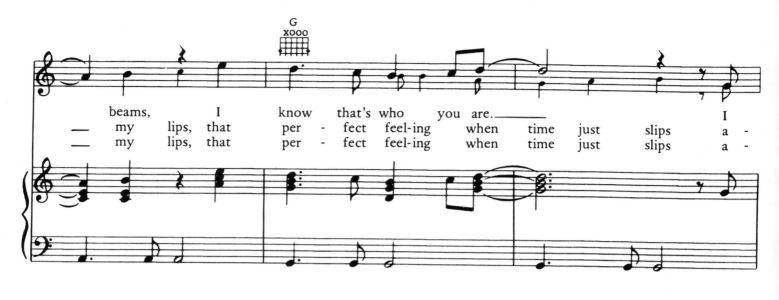

beams,　　I　know　that's　who　you　are.＿＿＿＿　　　　I
— my　lips,　that　per - fect　feel-ing　when　time　just　slips　　　a a -
— my　lips,　that　per - fect　feel-ing　when　time　just　slips　　　a a -

saw　your　brown＿ eyes　turn-ing　once＿　to　fire.＿
way　be - tween＿ us　and　our　fog - gy　trips.＿
way　be - tween＿ us　and　our　fog - gy　trips.＿

You　are　like　a　hur - ri-cane:　there's　calm　in　your　eye.＿

STAR OF BETHLEHEM

Words and Music by
NEIL YOUNG

THE WILL TO LOVE

Words and Music by
NEIL YOUNG

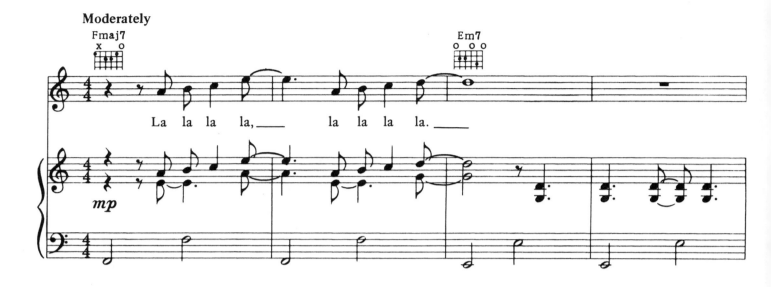

HOMEGROWN

Words and Music by
NEIL YOUNG

OLD COUNTRY WALTZ

Words and Music by
NEIL YOUNG

Moderate Country Waltz

They were play-ing that old coun-try waltz in this
loved, and I lost, and I cried the
play-ing it, that old coun-try waltz in this

emp-ty bar__ ech-o-ing off the wall.__ When I
day that the__ two of us__ died.__ Ain't
emp-ty bar__ ech-o-ing off the wall.__ Ain't

first got the bad news that you set me free, the
got no ex-cus-es; I just want to ride while the
got no ex-cus-es; we just want to play that

HOLD BACK THE TEARS

Words and Music by
NEIL YOUNG

SADDLE UP THE PALOMINO

Words by
NEIL YOUNG, TIM DRUMMOND
and BOBBY CHARLES

Music by
NEIL YOUNG

Oh, oh, Car - me - li - na, the
If you can't __ cut it,
I wan - na lick the __ plat - ter; the

daugh - ter of the wealth - y bank - er. Since she came to town __ all my
don't pick up the knife. __ There's no re - ward __ in your
gra - vy does - n't mat - ter. It's a cold bowl of chil - i when

141

HEY BABE!

Words and Music by
NEIL YOUNG

144

G
XOOO
can you see my love
E7
To Coda
1.
2. D. S. (lyric 1) al Coda
shin - ing for you? for you?
Coda
for you?
Repeat and fade
D
A
Em7
Hey, babe, I know that all things pass.
Repeat and fade
G
XOOO
A
D
Let's try to make this last. Hey, babe.

BITE THE BULLET

Words and Music by
NEIL YOUNG

146

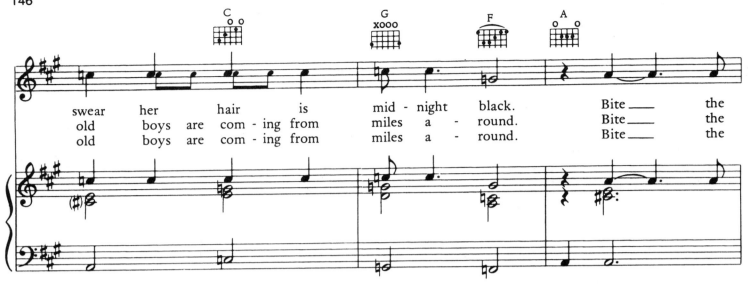

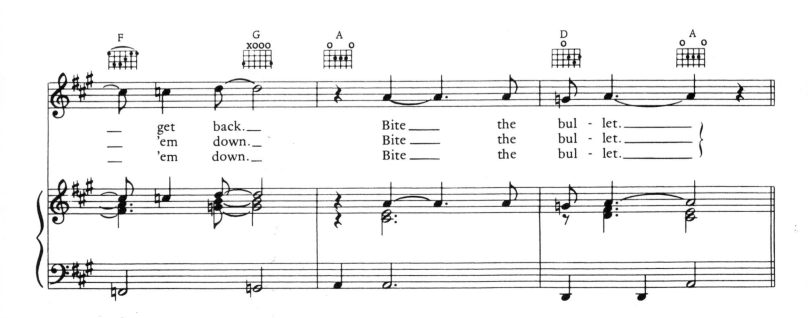

COMES A TIME

Birthday, November, 1977,
Miami.

COMES A TIME

Words and Music by
NEIL YOUNG

Comes a time____ when_ you're drift-in'.____
You and I,____ we____ were cap-tured.____

Comes a time____ when you set-tle down.__
We took our souls____ and we flew a-way.__

G Bm D Am7 C

GOIN' BACK

Words and Music by
NEIL YOUNG

LOOK OUT FOR MY LOVE

Words and Music by
NEIL YOUNG

ALREADY ONE

Words and Music by
NEIL YOUNG

What can I do, ____ what can I say, ____
Your laugh-ing eyes, ____ your cra-zy smile, ____
In my new life, ____ I'm trav-'lin' light, ____

run-nin' down ____ this sus-pi-cious high-way? ____
ev-'ry time ____ I look in his ____ face. ____
eyes wide o - pen for the next ____ move. ____

Now on-ly time___ can come be-tween _____ us, 'cause we're

al - read-y one.___ Our lit-tle son___ won't

let us___ for-get.___

RUST NEVER SLEEPS

Road-eyes move with purpose and fervor, 1979.

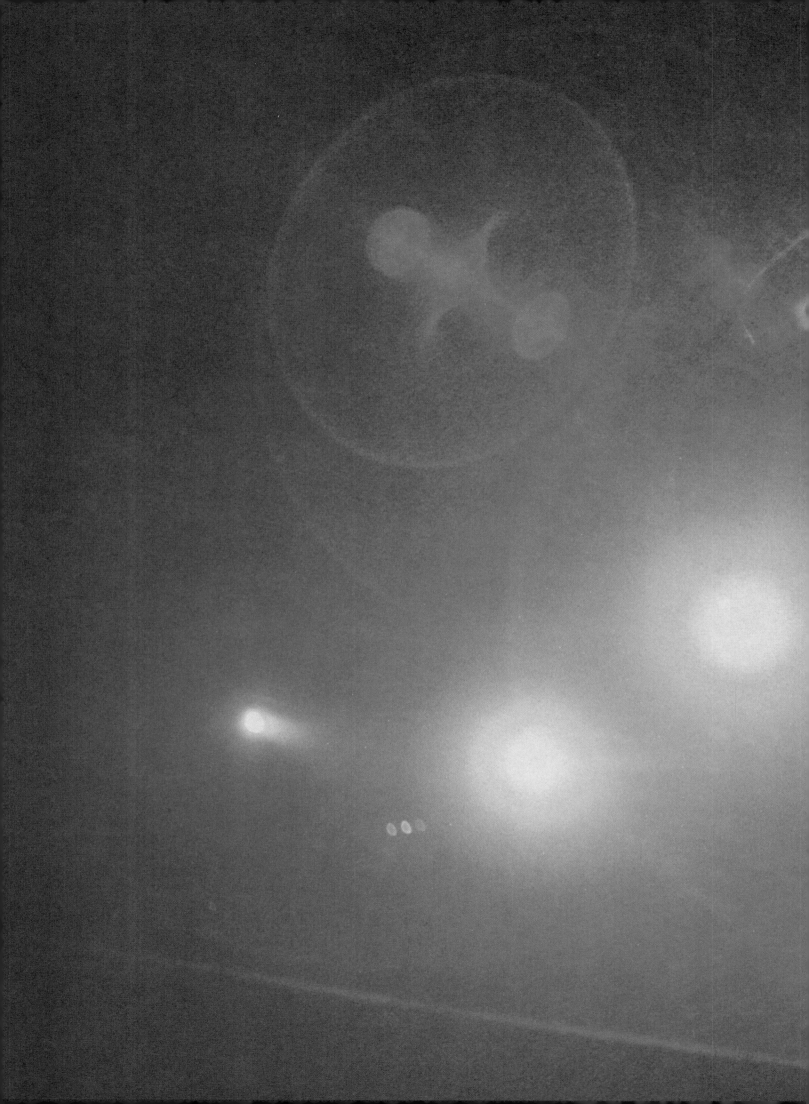

PEACE OF MIND

Words and Music by
NEIL YOUNG

FIELD OF OPPORTUNITY

Words and Music by
NEIL YOUNG

Moderate Country style

I been wrong be-fore, __ and I'll be there __ a-gain. __
go-in' back to my house, but I'm not go - in' now. __
all done cul-ti-vat-in', I'll be rock-in' on the porch, __

I don't have __ an-y an - swers, __ my friend,
It's too ear - ly to be leav - in' here, some - how.
tryin' __ to pic-ture you __ and where you are.

LOTTA LOVE

Words and Music by
NEIL YOUNG

MOTORCYCLE MAMA

Words and Music by
NEIL YOUNG

Mo - tor - cy - cle Ma - ma, won't you lay your big___ spike down?___

Mo - tor - cy - cle Ma - ma, won't you

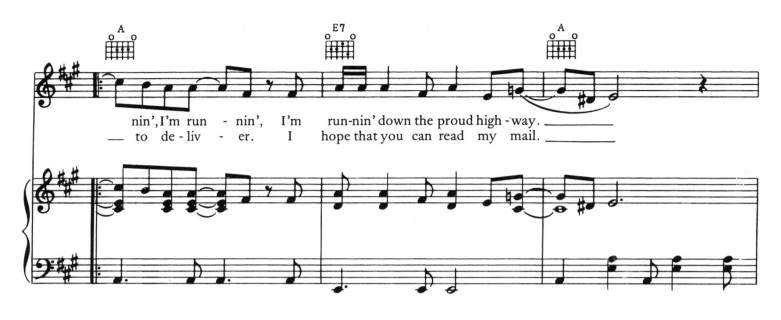

nin', I'm run - nin', I'm run-nin' down the proud high - way. _____
___ to de - liv - er. I hope that you can read my mail. _____

Yeah, I'm run - nin', I'm run - nin', I'm run-nin' down that proud high - way. _
I just es - caped last _ night _ from the Mem-o - ry Coun - ty Jail. _

_____ And as long _____ as I ___ keep mov-
_____ I see your box is o - pen and your flag _

HUMAN HIGHWAY

Words and Music by
NEIL YOUNG

DECADE

Backstage at the
Boarding House,
May, 1978.

THE CAMPAIGNER

Words and Music by
NEIL YOUNG

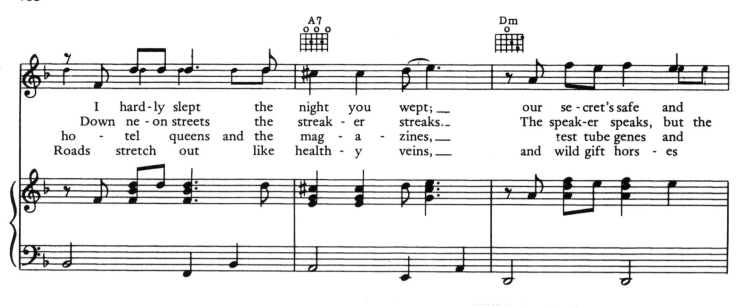

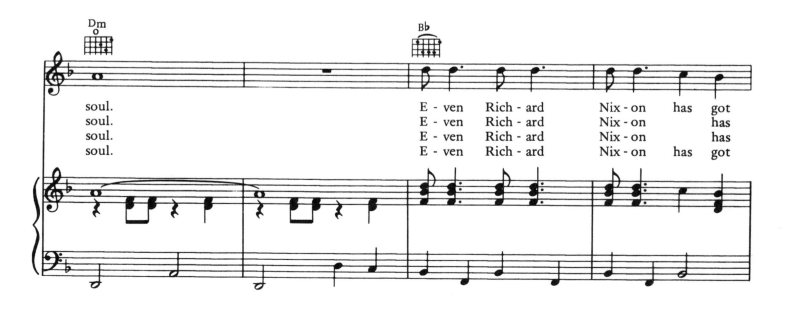

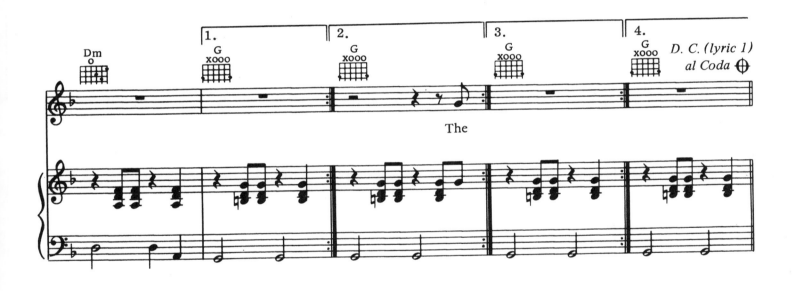

DEEP FORBIDDEN LAKE

Words and Music by
NEIL YOUNG

LOVE IS A ROSE

Words and Music by
NEIL YOUNG

DOWN TO THE WIRE

Words and Music by
NEIL YOUNG

Moderately, with a beat

WINTERLONG

Words and Music by
NEIL YOUNG

Moderately, with a beat

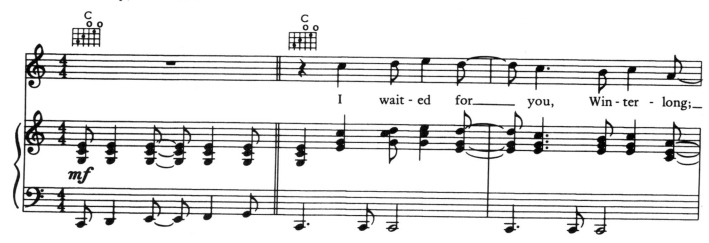

I wait-ed for____ you, Win - ter - long;____

____ you seem to be ____ where I be - long.____ It's all il - lu -

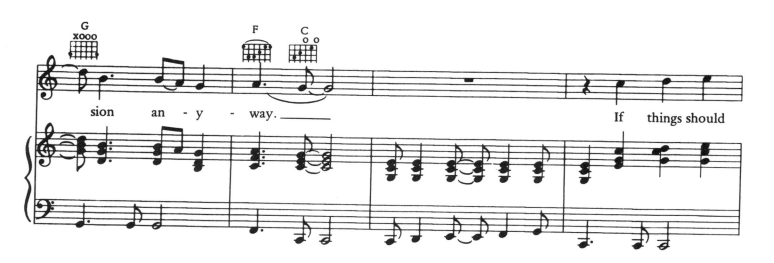

sion an - y - way. ____ If things should

Curtain call, 1979.

MY MY, HEY HEY
(OUT OF THE BLUE)

Words and Music by
NEIL YOUNG and JEFF BLACKBURN

My, my, hey, hey. _____
Out of the blue _____ and in-to the black. _____
The king is gone _____ but he's not for-got - ten.

Rock-and - roll is here to stay. _____
They give you this but you pay for that. _____
This is the sto - ry of John-ny Rot - ten.

* Guitarists: Tune all strings down one whole step.

SAIL AWAY

Words and Music by
NEIL YOUNG

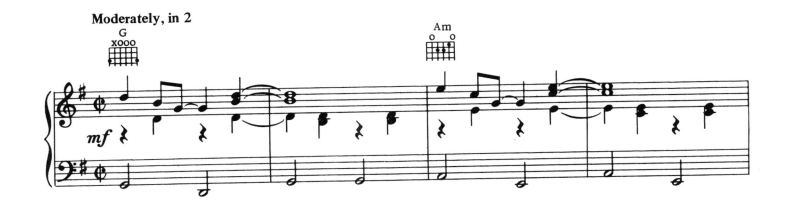

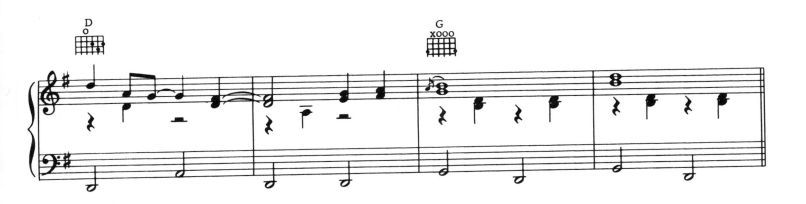

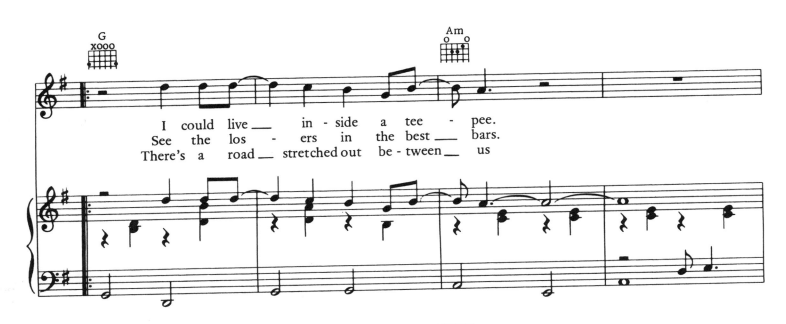

I could live ___ in - side a tee - pee.
See the los - ers in the best ___ bars.
There's a road ___ stretched out be - tween ___ us

THRASHER

Words and Music by
NEIL YOUNG

try-in' to catch an hour __ on __ the sun, __ when I

saw those thrash-ers roll-in' by __ look-in' more than two __ lanes wide. __

I was feel-in' like __ my day _____ had just be-gun. __

2. Where the

2. Where the eagle glides descending, there's an ancient river bending
Through the timeless gorge of changes where sleeplessness awaits.
I searched out my companions, who were lost in crystal canyons,
When the aimless blade of science slashed the pearly gates.
It was then that I knew I'd had enough; burned my credit card for fuel,
Headed out to where the pavement turns to sand,
With a one-way ticket to the land of truth and my suitcase in my hand.
How I lost my friends I still don't understand.

3. They had the best selection; they were poisoned with protection.
There was nothing that they needed, nothing left to find.
They were lost in rock formations or became park bench mutations.
On the sidewalks and in the stations, they were waiting, waiting.
So I got bored and left them there, they were just dead weight to me.
Better down the road without that load.
Brings back the time when I was eight or nine,
I was watchin' my mama's TV. It was that great Grand Canyon rescue episode.

4. Where the vulture glides descending, on an asphalt highway bending,
Through libraries and museums, galaxies and stars,
Down the windy halls of friendship to the rose clipped by the bullwhip,
The motel of lost companions waits with heated pool and bar.
But me, I'm not stopping there; got my own row left to hoe,
Just another line in the field of time.
When the thrasher comes I'll be stuck in the sun like dinosaurs in shrines,
But I'll know the time has come to give what's mine.

RIDE MY LLAMA

Words and Music by
NEIL YOUNG

Moderately, in 2

Re - mem-ber the Al - a - mo _____ when help was on _ the way. _ It's bet - ter here _ and now; _ I

214

POWDERFINGER

Words and Music by
NEIL YOUNG

2. Daddy's gone and my brother's out huntin' in the mountains.
   Big John's been drinkin' since the river took Emmy Lou.
   So the powers that be left me here to do the thinkin'.
   And I just turned twenty-two. I was wonderin' what to do.
   And the closer they got, the more those feelin's grew.

3. Daddy's rifle in my hand felt reassurin'.
   He told me, "Red means run, Son. Numbers add up to nothin'."
   But when the first shot hit the dock, I saw it comin'.
   Raised my rifle to my eye. Never stopped to wonder why.
   Then I saw black and my face flash in the sky.

4. Shelter me from the powder and the finger.
   Cover me with the thought that pulled the trigger.
   Just think of me as one you never figured.
   You fade away so young, with so much left undone.
   Remember me to my love. I know I'll miss her.

POCOHANTUS

Words and Music by
NEIL YOUNG

2. They killed us in our teepee and they cut our women down.
They might have left some babies cryin' on the ground.
But the fire stays and the wagons come,
And the night falls on the settin' sun.

3. They massacred the buffalo kitty-corner from the bank.
And the taxis run across my feet, and my eyes have turned to blanks.
And my little box at the top of the stairs
With my Indian rug and a pipe to share.

4. I wish I was a trapper. I would give a thousand pelts
To sleep with Pocohantus and find out how she felt
In the mornin' on the fields of green,
In the homeland we've never seen.

5. And maybe Marlon Brando will be there by the fire.
We'll sit and talk of Hollywood and the good things there for hire
And the Astrodome and the first teepee,
Marlon Brando, Pocohantus and me. Pocohantus.

WELFARE MOTHERS

Words and Music by
NEIL YOUNG

HEY HEY, MY MY
(INTO THE BLACK)

Words and Music by
NEIL YOUNG

Medium Rock beat

Hey, hey, my, my.
Out of the blue and in - to the black.
The king is gone but he's not for - got - ten.

Rock - and - roll can nev - er die.
You pay for this but they give you that.
Is this the sto - ry of John - ny Rot -

SEDAN DELIVERY

Words and Music by
NEIL YOUNG

Moderate Rock beat, in 2

Last night I was cool __ at the pool __ hall.

Held the ta-ble for e - lev-en games. __ Noth-ing was eas - i - er than __

__ the first sev - en. I beat a wom-an with var - i-cose veins.